Meditations in the desert

A group study course exploring the story of Moses

Patrick Coghlan

kevin mayhew

kevin mayhew

First published in Great Britain in 2008 by Kevin Mayhew Ltd
Buxhall, Stowmarket, Suffolk IP14 3BW
Tel: +44 (0) 1449 737978 Fax: +44 (0) 1449 737834
E-mail: info@kevinmayhewltd.com

www.kevinmayhew.com

© 2008 Patrick Coghlan

The right of Patrick Coghlan to be identified as the author of this work has been asserted by him in accordance with the Copyright, Designs and Patents Act 1988.

All rights reserved. No part of this publication may be reproduced, stored in a retrieval system, or transmitted, in any form or by any means, electronic, mechanical, photocopying, recording or otherwise, without the prior written permission of the publisher.

9 8 7 6 5 4 3 2 1 0

ISBN 978 1 84417 9473
Catalogue No. 1501077

Cover design by Rob Mortonson
Edited and typeset by Katherine Laidler

Printed and bound in Great Britain

Contents

Introduction		5
Managing the sessions		7
Moses: My story		9
Session 1	Grumbling against God	11
Session 2	God's provision	15
Session 3	The importance of prayer	19
Session 4	Supporting our spiritual leaders	23
Session 5	Witnessing to others	27
Session 6	God's law	31
Summary	What is your response?	35

About the author

Patrick Coghlan is the pastor of Worstead Baptist Church in Norfolk. He has considerable experience of working with all age groups, both in the Church and in the wider community. As a Baptist minister, he provides pastoral care and teaching, regularly takes school assemblies, leads a monthly service at a sheltered housing scheme and is actively involved with a Christian community care charity.

He is also a trained Christian counsellor and an enthusiastic author. *Friday Evening Bible Study*, *Letters Pray*, *Loved Without Condition*, *Roger's Diary* and *Stories To Perform* are all published by Kevin Mayhew.

Patrick is married to June. They have two children, Rachel and Jonathan.

Introduction

Meditations in the Desert is the fifth in a series of six studies looking at various Bible characters and what lessons we can learn from them. The other books in the series are *Meditations in the Garden* (Adam and Eve), *Meditations on a Boat* (Noah), *Meditations on a Journey* (Abraham), *Meditations in Captivity* (Joseph) and *Meditations in the Body* (Jesus). Each of the studies is self-contained and written in a similar format. Together, they comprise a progressive course of study – each following on from the previous one but individually still bringing out a variety of different spiritual lessons.

Meditations in the Desert looks at Moses. There are six sessions, each concentrating on a different aspect of his story. The **Summary** at the end of the book is provided partly as homework and partly as a seventh session with a social focus. It is a personal and collective response to the study – how this applies to me, how this applies to my fellowship, and how this applies to the Church as a whole. The study is written in such a way as to encourage group participation in a number of different ways, including discussion, researching background knowledge and prayer. The material is imaginative, sometimes humorous, but also scripturally based and challenging, encouraging each member of the group to seek prayerfully what God is saying to them today, through Scripture – and then to apply it.

Each study in the series has a number of component parts:

Moses: My story is an introduction to the story of Moses (based on Exodus 1:1–40:38). It is presented in the format of a short autobiography. This, together with the Bible passage on which the course is based (Exodus 15:22–20:26), should be read at home in preparation for the start of the course.

The **Opening prayer** may be used as given, or members of the group could be asked to take it in turns to prepare an alternative.

The **Icebreaker**, though light-hearted and intended to help the group relax and begin to gel together, has relevance to the overall theme of the session. It is sometimes a whole group activity and sometimes carried out in smaller groups or pairs.

In the section headed **As a group**, the theme introduced in the previous section is developed a little further. It may involve feedback to the whole group.

The **Introduction to the session** involves a time of meditation, in preparation for the Bible reading and time of analysis, discussion and application. It may take the form of prose, verse or a short sketch. This is an opportunity for members of the group to take part in reading or acting.

The **Bible reference** section is in two parts. The part entitled **Based on** gives details of the overall passage of Scripture on which the particular session is based (this will have been read at home in preparation for the course). However, this may be too long to read through in the session; when that is the case, **Read** gives a shorter, more specific Bible passage. A member of the group may be chosen to do the reading or a volunteer asked for. You may even choose to read it from more than one different version of the Bible.

Discussion is encouraged by posing a series of statements and questions around the theme, and relating to the passage of Scripture that the session has been based on: its background, content and application. Some additional related passages are linked into the discussion time.

The **Closing prayer** may be read by one of the group. However, once again, a member of the group could be asked in advance to prepare an alternative prayer, or there could be a time of open prayer.

Managing the sessions

Each member of the group should be encouraged to have their own copy of *Meditations in the Desert* to facilitate following the course and, more importantly, to enable them to perform the tasks for individual reflection – in particular, the personal responses in the **Summary** at the end of the book. Also, there may be occasions when it is necessary for participants to bring in visual aids – for example, for the **Icebreaker** exercise: the book is their prompt.

It is a good idea for the members of the group to keep a personal journal during the course, including their responses to the sessions, action points, prayer needs and anything else that is appropriate.

It is important that the sessions be conducted with sensitivity and bearing in mind practical issues such as seating arrangements and safety. Without blocking access to exits, seating should be arranged in such a way that people can easily move from a single group into pairs or small groups. An OHP or a flipchart needs to be placed where people can see it clearly, when required. Also an area needs to be left clear for acting out the sketches, or for a TV and video/DVD player if a sketch has been pre-recorded. Suitable arrangements need to be made for the serving of any refreshments.

It may be helpful to have some Christian music playing softly in the background as people arrive, and perhaps to offer a soft drink – this will encourage participants to relax and unwind but, at the same time, begin to focus on a meditative time of study. A short time of silence just before the **Opening prayer** can be very helpful, allowing people to focus on God. The leader needs to be sensitive to the movement of the study; indeed, there may be other occasions when a time of quiet, personal prayer or reflection is appropriate. For example, after the **Introduction to the session** a time of personal reflection could be helpful; and following the discussion time, members of the group may want to spend a few minutes jotting down notes of response in their journals before the final prayer.

Timing of the session is very important. The group should determine a finishing time in advance of the session and should stick to it as closely as possible – it is not a good idea to allow sessions to be open-ended. Try to start on time. Keep the **Icebreaker** and **As a group** sections fairly short (approximately four minutes for the **Icebreaker** and eight minutes for **As a group**). The length of time allocated for **Discussion** will be determined by your finishing time. The leader's aim should be to encourage one section to flow smoothly into the next, but there may be occasions when they will need to interrupt the proceedings sensitively in order to move things on.

Confidentiality should be respected within the group, to promote a safe and trusting environment.

One or two suitable people should be available to provide ministry at the end of each session. If this is not practical, the group leader should know who to direct people to if an issue arises which they are unable to deal with.

Moses

The Autobiography

What, you might ask, was an Israelite doing growing up in the Egyptian Pharaoh's palace? When I was born, a law had been passed stating that all the Israelite baby boys should be killed at birth. What unbelievable cruelty!

Mum wasn't having any of that – so I was told. Having prevented me from being killed at birth, a short time after she suddenly announced to the whole family, 'It's no good, we can't hide a growing child for much longer, but I've got an idea.'

Dad was sceptical: 'That's ridiculous. It will never work.'

But it did. I was put into a waterproof basket, and floated up the river to where the Egyptian princess always bathed.

'Oh look,' she cried out, 'a baby. Take it back to the palace. I shall bring him up as my own.'

My sister was close at hand, and volunteered Mother to be my nanny. Of course, the princess didn't know that she was my mum! And the offer was accepted.

I grew up in the royal palace in the lap of luxury, but, at the same time, I learned about my own culture. When I grew up and saw how badly the Egyptian slave masters were treating the Israelites, I became angry. I caught one of the Egyptians beating a slave; I was unable to control my rage any longer... and killed him.

I was so frightened that I ran away to Midian. While I was there, I was married to Zipporah and we had a son. And then...well, a strange thing happened. I saw a burning bush that technically wasn't burning. The flames were there, but they didn't consume the bush. And that's where God spoke to me. He told me to take off my sandals because the ground was holy.

'I've got a job for you, Moses.'

It all became clear to me: why God had saved me from being slaughtered as a baby and why I was taken to the palace. God wanted me to lead the Israelite slaves out of captivity.

'They're going to like that,' I thought to myself. 'I'll soon be Mr Popular with the Egyptians – I don't think! Besides, it's not really my gifting.'

I was reluctant to take on the task, but God told me that my brother Aaron would help. First of all, we had to go and speak to Pharaoh. Then God sent all kinds of plagues to the Egyptians, after which they still only let the Israelites go with great reluctance. What's more, the soldiers chased after us, and it was only through a watery miracle of God that we were saved.

We'd hardly left Egypt before the moaning started...Why do people do that?

'We were better off in Egypt,' they whinged. But they weren't...not really!

And that was the beginning of years living in the wilderness and desert, as we travelled to the Promised Land. Although, I don't think any of us expected it to take this long. I'm an old man now, and we're still not there.

Session 1
Grumbling against God

Opening prayer

Heavenly Father,
thank you that you shower us with your love
in so many different ways:
providing for our needs,
guiding and strengthening us in our weakness,
and providing the way back to you through Jesus.

*(Spend some time in silent prayer thanking God
for some of the expressions of his love that you benefit from.)*

Be with us during this study of Moses.
Fill us afresh with your Holy Spirit
and help us to learn prayerfully more about you
and your purposes.
Make our response a positive one.
In Jesus' name.
Amen.

Icebreaker

Leylandii hedges, dripping taps, dirty washing left on the bathroom floor . . . In pairs, without taking this too seriously, what kind of things do you love to grumble about?

As a group

Using an OHP or a flipchart, have a brainstorming session on what you understand by the words 'ungrateful' and 'fickle'. Give some hypothetical examples of both.

Introduction to the session

Meditation – How Moses might have expressed his frustration about the people's grumbling in the desert

Nothing but moan, moan, moan . . .
Whinge, whinge, whinge . . .
'We're thirsty!'
'We're hungry!'
Why can't they see how good God has been to them in bringing them out of slavery? Why do they turn round and say that they were better off in Egypt? I saw how they suffered under the hands of their slave masters.

To think I was brought up as a prince in a palace. I was respected, powerful . . . and now I have to contend with this constant grumbling against me and against God. Whatever happened to gratitude? Such a fickle crowd!

Why can't they be more positive? I'm sure they would feel better if they were thankful about what God has done and still is doing for them, instead of moaning about every little difficulty we go through.

God will provide – we just need to have faith, and a little bit of patience.

Bible references

- Based on Exodus 15:22–20:26
- Read Exodus 15:22-27, 16:2-3 and 17:1-3

Discussion

- During the grumbles of the people in the desert, God instructs them to listen to him, do what is right in his sight and obey his commandments. He links this with the promise of being free from the diseases that the Egyptians suffered from. Maybe there is an obvious connection: to some extent we can be our own worst enemies – for example, eating incorrectly can cause health problems, promiscuous lifestyles can lead to disease. Discuss.

- It is easy to blame someone else for our problems – even God. But God does not instigate suffering, pain, problems or hardship, although sometimes he allows it for a purpose. Discuss.

- The Israelites seem to be all set to turn round and head back into Egyptian captivity. It is easy to give up when the going gets difficult. Talk about this in the light of Jesus' statement in Luke 9:62.

- Moses and the people seem to be pulling in different spiritual directions. Deuteronomy 22:10 speaks about not yoking animals unequally. Later on in the Bible (2 Corinthians 6:14) Paul emphasises the importance of this concept in a spiritual sense, linked with marriage. What does it mean to be unequally yoked in a spiritual context, and what are the likely consequences?

- 1 Chronicles 16:8 tells us to give thanks to God for his goodness and to tell others. It is easy to grumble, but it is not uplifting like giving thanks. What do you think?

Closing prayer

Generous heavenly Father,
thank you for your continued provision to us,
as an expression of your love.
Help us to take care of the world in which we live
and to share what we have with others.
When we are tempted to grumble,
encourage us to think about all the ways
in which you have blessed us.
Give us the strength and focus not to lose heart and give up
while serving Jesus in fulfilling our calling.

Make our marriages and family relationships strong
by uniting us in our Christian faith.
Be with and help those who are less fortunate than us.
In Jesus' name.
Amen.

Session 2
God's provision

Opening prayer

Heavenly Father,
thank you that you shower us with your love
in so many different ways:
providing for our needs,
guiding and strengthening us in our weakness,
and providing the way back to you through Jesus.

*(Spend some time in silent prayer thanking God
for some of the expressions of his love that you benefit from.)*

Be with us during this study of Moses.
Fill us afresh with your Holy Spirit
and help us to learn prayerfully more about you
and your purposes.
Make our response a positive one.
In Jesus' name.
Amen.

Icebreaker

In pairs, using a selection of catalogues and brochures, try to differentiate between the things we need and those that are luxuries or even sheer extravagance. If you are feeling artistic, cut some pictures out and make a collage of the three categories.

As a group

To what extent does the type of society we live in dictate our needs? Discuss.

Introduction to the session

Meditation – What one of the Israelites might have said about God's provision of food

It will be time to go out and get bread soon. We have to collect extra today, because tomorrow is the Sabbath and there won't be any to collect then. The funny thing is that the bread we collect for the Sabbath keeps completely fresh, and yet, if we gather extra at any other time, it goes mouldy and smelly. You see, God wants us to bring in only what we need – no more and no less! It's very tempting to try and stock up, just in case God accidentally forgets or something. But that's just what he doesn't want us to do. God wants us to learn to be obedient and trust in his provision – one day at a time. I have to say that he hasn't let us down yet. We call the bread manna. It's amazing how each morning it arrives with the dew.

I know we gave Moses and Aaron a hard time ... and, well, they were doing their best. They can't be expected to do everything, be all things to all people, you know. It wasn't really fair the way we treated them.

I wonder how many more weeks we will be stuck in the desert. I sincerely hope it won't be too long! Although this journey has given me a new perspective on life: sometimes the things we think we need aren't always very important at all.

Bible references

- Based on Exodus 15:22–20:26
- Read Exodus 16:1-36

Discussion

- The people grumble at Moses and Aaron. It is so easy to grumble to our church leaders. Talk about positive and negative criticism.

- Suddenly the people begin to paint a rosy picture of Egypt. They refer to being brought into the desert to starve. When times are hard, it is easy to look at the past with rose-tinted glasses. Do you think the Israelites really want to be back in Egypt? How do we move forward at times like this?

- God responds to the moaning by providing quail in the evening and bread (manna) from heaven in the morning. What characteristics of God does this illustrate?

- The instruction that comes with the bread is to gather enough for one day at a time (except on the sixth day when double should be collected). God does this to test the people. Discuss and relate to life in the twenty-first century.

- Moses instructs the Israelites not to keep any of the bread for the next morning. However, some disobey and it goes maggoty and smelly, although that which is kept overnight for the seventh (Sabbath) day keeps fresh. Some also disobey by going out on the Sabbath to gather bread, but there is none. What does this say about the relationship between obedience and blessing?

- God provides bread for the Israelites for forty years, until they enter Canaan. In John 6:25-40 Jesus refers back to this, and goes on to speak about himself as the bread of life. What does he mean by this? How does this teaching apply to us today?

Closing prayer

God who provides,
thank you for all the good gifts that you give to us in your love.
Help us to be grateful to you and generous with others.
Teach us to deal responsibly with the resources you provide.
Give us the kind of hearts
that focus on your continued faithfulness to us.
Thank you for Jesus, who is able to nourish us in a spiritual sense.

Fill us with the desire to follow him more closely
and allow the Holy Spirit to work within our lives,
cleansing and transforming us.
In Jesus' name.
Amen.

Session 3
The importance of prayer

Opening prayer

Heavenly Father,
thank you that you shower us with your love
in so many different ways:
providing for our needs,
guiding and strengthening us in our weakness,
and providing the way back to you through Jesus.

*(Spend some time in silent prayer thanking God
for some of the expressions of his love that you benefit from.)*

Be with us during this study of Moses.
Fill us afresh with your Holy Spirit
and help us to learn prayerfully more about you
and your purposes.
Make our response a positive one.
In Jesus' name.
Amen.

Icebreaker

In pairs, talk about when and where you pray. Make a list of what you consider to be the important elements of prayer. Then, individually, write on a small piece of paper something to thank God for and a request, and fold up the paper. Place all of these into a small basket to be prayed over later. These remain confidential between the writer and God, and should be destroyed later.

As a group

Discuss your findings about the important elements of prayer.

Introduction to the session

Sketch – Moses reaches out to God

> *The scene: Moses standing on the stage, with the voice of God coming from offstage.*

Moses They're moaning again: this time they want water. They blame me, you know. What am I going to do? I told you that it wasn't a good idea for me to be leading them. Things are getting nasty, tempers are getting frayed. I have fears for my safety if I can't deliver some water. What am I saying? That's putting it mildly: they are almost ready to stone me. You have to help me. I need your protection, power and provision . . . and I need patience, perseverance and . . . and . . . and a sense of humour.

Voice of God Here comes your brother; I think he wants something.

Aaron *(Approaches Moses)* Moses?

Moses Can't you see I'm busy?

Aaron I'm sorry, but the people are thirsty. What are we going to do?

Moses I'm dealing with it.

Aaron You need to be quick; they're beginning to turn nasty.

Moses Beginning to . . . *(Addressing God)* What are we going to do? Where will we find water here?

Voice of God *(Trying to calm Moses down)* Try not to be so anxious, Moses. Have I ever let you down? Haven't I always done what I said I would do? I provided food, didn't I?

Moses *(Humbled)* I admit you've never let me down.

Voice of God Use the staff again. Take some of the other leaders to the rock at Horeb. Strike the rock with the staff and water will come out.

Moses   Thanks, God. You could have just saved my life here – literally! *(Turns in the direction of the people)* COME ON, YOU LOT. FOLLOW US. WE'RE ALL GOING FOR A LONG COOL DRINK!

Voice of God   Oh, by the way, Moses . . . I'll think about the sense of humour!

Bible references

- Based on Exodus 15:22–20:26
- Read Exodus 17:1-7

Discussion

- It is not an easy time for the Israelites as they travel across barren desert. Imagine being desperately thirsty, tired, unsettled . . . Though we may not experience living in the wilderness in a physical sense, there could well be times when we experience it in a spiritual sense – when our walk with Jesus seems to be hard work; when we struggle to understand what he wants us to do; when we push doors that seem to remain firmly closed; when prayer and worship don't seem to come easily. Discuss, with particular reference to the possible causes of such times, how we should deal with them.

- Moses cries out to God in despair. Some people only cry out to God when things are going wrong, using prayer as a last resort. Some are reluctant to bring their own needs to God at all. Some treat prayer as an intrinsic part of everyday life. Discuss.

- God provides the Israelites with water, but only after Moses has followed his instructions. Think of some hypothetical situations in which God uses men, women and children to fulfil his purposes – even to the extent of performing the miraculous.

- If Moses hadn't listened, he wouldn't have heard God's instructions and the Israelites wouldn't have had water to drink. Discuss with relevance to us today.

- Talk about the prayer that Jesus teaches in Matthew 6:9-13. Compare with your earlier findings about the important elements of prayer.

- Why do we need to be persistent in prayer? After all, God loves to give us good gifts (Luke 11:5-13).

Closing prayer

Our Father in heaven,
thank you that you love to hear our prayers,
and that you answer them
in the way that is best for us and your purposes for creation –
even when you say 'no' or 'wait'.
Thank you that you share with us in the hard times
as well as the good.
Grant us faith, patience and perseverance in prayer.
Help us to make time for prayer, even in the busyness of our days.

(Holding the basket of prayers from earlier)

You know our hearts and minds,
including the things that concern us.
We bring to you these prayers of thanksgiving and these requests,
and place them into your hands.
In Jesus' name.
Amen.

Session 4
Supporting our spiritual leaders

Opening prayer

Heavenly Father,
thank you that you shower us with your love
in so many different ways:
providing for our needs,
guiding and strengthening us in our weakness,
and providing the way back to you through Jesus.

*(Spend some time in silent prayer thanking God
for some of the expressions of his love that you benefit from.)*

Be with us during this study of Moses.
Fill us afresh with your Holy Spirit
and help us to learn prayerfully more about you
and your purposes.
Make our response a positive one.
In Jesus' name.
Amen.

Icebreaker

Talk about ways in which you could show your appreciation to the leadership of your church fellowship for all that they do – for example, a 'thank you' card, a gift, an invitation to dinner, mowing their lawns. Maybe you could give them some words of encouragement. So, what *are* you going to do about it?

As a group

What are the strengths of the leadership of your fellowship? Make a list.

Introduction to the session

Meditation – In leadership

Being a leader demands certain qualities, such as having a strong faith in Jesus, being filled with the Holy Spirit, having a good listening ear to what God is saying, possessing wisdom to make decisions and offer advice, being able to lead through example, having vision and the ability to inspire others to share in that vision, and, at the end of the day, being willing to carry the onus of spiritual responsibility. Entering into leadership in the Church is a calling – one which should be tested.

There is a saying, 'It is lonely at the top'. It is not easy carrying the responsibility of church leadership. Often, when things are going well, nothing is said; but as soon as anything goes wrong, or the leadership fails to follow traditions or expectations, criticism can be quick and harsh.

Sometimes the leadership is expected to be all things to all people: leading worship, teaching, performing pastoral care, leading the young people's work, administration, organising care for the fabric and, if possible, filling any other gaps in church duties.

Though the role of leadership is not taken on for praise, a word of appreciation and encouragement is always gratefully received and goes a long way! An offer to carry the burden of some of the more practical roles provides the relief to focus more on spiritual ones. Exodus 17.8-16 is a wonderful illustration of offering this kind of support to our spiritual leaders.

Bible references

- Based on Exodus 15:22–20:26
- Read Exodus 17:8-16

Discussion

- The Israelites face a physical battle. Talk about the spiritual battle which faces the Christian Church.

- In Exodus 4:1-5, before we joined Moses' story, God tells Moses to use his staff in a special way. In Exodus 17:6, God tells Moses to strike the rock with his staff. Now, in Exodus 17:8-16, Moses stands at the top of the hill with the same staff, as Joshua leads an army into battle. Talk about the significance of the staff. Are there modern equivalents in churches today?

- Moses' act of holding his hands up is a prayerful position and therefore denotes looking to God for help in battle. It is God's desire that we should look to him for guidance and strength, but we don't always do that. Discuss.

- Moses prays on behalf of those in battle. Talk about mediating for others in prayer, with particular reference to Jesus mediating for us (1 Timothy 2:5).

- Aaron and Hur hold Moses' arms in the air as he begins to get tired. What does this say about doing practical things to take some of the pressure off our church leaders?

- What does 1 Timothy chapter 3 have to say about the qualities required to be a church leader?

Closing prayer

Lord Jesus,
you are the head, and we are your body
at work in the world today.
Guide us in all things, through the Holy Spirit.
Empower and equip us to face the spiritual battle
that is going on in the world today.
Protect us from the powers of evil.

We pray especially for those who have been called
to positions of leadership within the Church:
may they be filled with your strength and wisdom
as they lead your people.
Help us to respect those in leadership
and provide them with the support that they need and are due.
Give us positive and encouraging words that are constructive,
rather than those that hurt or discourage.
Forgive us for the times when we have,
intentionally or unintentionally,
failed to be supportive.
In Jesus' name.
Amen.

Session 5
Witnessing to others

Opening prayer

Heavenly Father,
thank you that you shower us with your love
in so many different ways:
providing for our needs,
guiding and strengthening us in our weakness,
and providing the way back to you through Jesus.

*(Spend some time in silent prayer thanking God
for some of the expressions of his love that you benefit from.)*

Be with us during this study of Moses.
Fill us afresh with your Holy Spirit
and help us to learn prayerfully more about you
and your purposes.
Make our response a positive one.
In Jesus' name.
Amen.

Icebreaker

In pairs, take it in turns to look in a mirror and describe what you see (without being too critical). Then summarise what you think are your positive qualities (without being too modest).

As a group

What do others see? Talk about the qualities of Jesus that we seek to emulate in our own lives, for others to see and experience.

Introduction to the session

Meditation – What Jethro might have said retrospectively about visiting Moses in the desert

I have to admit, I am quite impressed with the way my son-in-law Moses has led the Israelites out of Egypt and into the desert. Through his leadership, God has done some amazing things with them. It was good to see Moses again, and I know Zipporah and the children were pleased to see him.

Moses was looking very tired, though, and it didn't take long to see why.

'You can't keep on like this,' I told him. 'For your own health, you need to delegate the job of settling disputes amongst the people . . . but you also need to teach people more about God and his ways, so that they are not so dependent on the guidance of others – lead by example always!'

God wants a people who will be witnesses of his love and power to save. A people to be seen by other nations of the world.

He's a good son-in-law. He listened with humility, and then immediately put into action the things I advised.

Bible references

- Based on Exodus 15:22–20:26
- Read Exodus 18:1-27

Discussion

- Moses tells Jethro about the wonderful things that God has done for the Israelites. One strand of witness is about telling others what God has done for us. Discuss.

- Jethro helps Moses to devise a system of leadership that will encourage the Israelites to live according to God's standards.

The other strand of witness is 'being'. In other words, living the kind of lives that point to God. Discuss.

- The way Jethro offers advice to Moses is not confrontational, negative or judgemental. What effect can being judgemental have on our witness to others?

- Moses humbly accepts and acts upon the advice he is given. Talk about receiving advice with humility, and the importance of Christians working together as part of the witness of the Church.

- The Body of Christ is an illustration of what it means for the Church to be in unity and working together for God's purposes – looking to Jesus as the head (1 Corinthians 12:12-31). Discuss.

Closing prayer

Loving heavenly Father,
we thank you for the privilege
of being part of a worshipping, witnessing community
of your people.
Help us to look to the example and teaching of Jesus,
to base our lives on Scripture and to be prayerful.
Fill us afresh with the Holy Spirit
to cleanse, guide, empower and transform us.
Enable us to be the people you would have us be.
Help us to say and do only the things that are pleasing to you.
Give us the courage to tell others about our faith
and the empowerment to live it out on a daily basis.
Make us your witnesses to our families, at work,
in our social lives and in our neighbourhoods.
In Jesus' name.
Amen.

Session 6
God's law

Opening prayer

Heavenly Father,
thank you that you shower us with your love
in so many different ways:
providing for our needs,
guiding and strengthening us in our weakness,
and providing the way back to you through Jesus.

*(Spend some time in silent prayer thanking God
for some of the expressions of his love that you benefit from.)*

Be with us during this study of Moses.
Fill us afresh with your Holy Spirit
and help us to learn prayerfully more about you
and your purposes.
Make our response a positive one.
In Jesus' name.
Amen.

Icebreaker

Have on display a flower arrangement, a box of chocolates, one or two other small gifts and some greetings cards. In pairs, discuss ways in which we express our love to each other (not just romantic love).

As a group

Talk about how God expresses his love to us.

Introduction to the session

Poem – The Ten Commandments

Ten simple rules from God above:
each an expression of his love;
all to enhance the lives we lead,
and help true freedom to succeed.

Rules one to three: his rightful place –
God our creator, full of grace.
Our number one priority:
before all things including 'ME'!

Rule four highlights our need for rest
and time with God, to be our best.
Rule number five involves respect:
care and compassion, not neglect.

To faithfulness and honesty,
and not to greed or jealousy,
we're called in seven, eight, nine, ten –
God's laws of love by his own pen.

There's number six to look at still,
which simply says, 'you must not kill.'
Much more implied than foul deed done . . .
to do no harm to anyone!

Bible references

- Based on Exodus 15:22–20:26
- Read Exodus 20:1-26

Discussion

- God's law is an expression of his love. Discuss.
- Talk about the modern idols that people allow to take the place of God in their lives. Can people be too comfortable to see their need for God?
- The modern attitude to Sundays is detrimental to physical and spiritual health – and family life. Discuss.
- A number of the Ten Commandments imply the need to have respect for each other. Which are they? In what contexts are we told to have that respect?
- Look at Matthew 5:17-20. What is Jesus saying in this passage?
- Talk about the way in which Jesus expands the Ten Commandments in the Sermon on the Mount (Matthew chapters 5-7).

Closing prayer

God of love,
thank you that, as an expression of your love,
you gave us your law:
for our own good and that of our families,
to bring peace and harmony to society,
and to further your kingdom.
Thank you that through Jesus
we can learn so much more about the law.
Grant us understanding of the meaning of the law;
give us the wisdom to recognise how to apply it;
and fill us with the courage and conviction to put it into practice.
Help us to be prepared to make a stand
for what we know to be right,
even to the extent of challenging the governments of the world.
In Jesus' name.
Amen.

Summary
Moses: What is your response?

Group response

Bring and share supper

Everyone is invited to bring something to eat or drink. The session begins with spending a relaxed time together over an informal meal. Maybe a few simple party games could be played after eating. Decorate the room with a selection of cacti and succulents to create the ambience of the desert.

Prayer

Say together:

Faithful God,
we thank you for your word, the Scriptures,
for their truth and relevance to us today.
Help us to understand what you have been saying to us
as we have been studying Moses' story,
and empower us to put those lessons into practice
in our daily lives.
Lead us forward in our individual Christian lives,
in the lives of the fellowship(s) we belong to
and as part of your Church as a whole.
Enable us to be a prayerful, scripturally based,
worshipping and witnessing people in the world around us –
starting with our families, neighbourhoods and workplaces.
In Jesus' name.
Amen.

Creative session

Using a flipchart or an OHP, pick out and list all the miracles of God contained within the story of Moses. Use these as the basis for making a banner illustrating the 'God of miracles'. (Some preparation may be done beforehand. If time runs out, complete the banner on another occasion.)

Remember the sessions

Session 1

Grumbling against God

God's commandments are for our own good, and the teaching of Jesus reinforces their importance to us. We must not be tempted to turn away from God and his purposes, even when the going gets tough. And it is good to remember that giving thanks is far more uplifting than grumbling.

Session 2

God's provision

God is faithful and he provides the things we need (even though we don't always share what we have). There is a strong link between obedience and blessing. But we need spiritual nourishment as well as physical nourishment: Jesus speaks about himself as being the 'bread of life'.

Session 3

The importance of prayer

Prayer should be an intrinsic part of everyday life. At times, when things are really hard, we can find ourselves really crying out to God in faith. We need to be persistent in prayer and listen to God's response. Remember, he loves to give good gifts.

Session 4

Supporting our spiritual leaders

We are in a spiritual battle for which we need God's help. Our spiritual leaders need our support and encouragement – even to the extent of providing practical help to free up more time for their spiritual tasks. Such leaders need to have special qualities.

Session 5

Witnessing to others

Followers of Jesus are called to be his witnesses in the world: in word and example. We should be loving and not judgemental, and the Church should be seen to be working together in unity and harmony.

Session 6

God's law

God's law is an expression of his love: it is for our benefit and that of his eternal purposes. He calls for our obedience to it.

Discussion

Talk about the application of the study of Moses with relevance to your church fellowship(s) and to the Church as a whole.

Prayer

Spend some time in open prayer, responding to what has been said.

Informal communion

If the group would like to, bring the session to a close by sharing bread and wine together.

Personal response

For individual reflection

Your own response to the story of Moses

Session 1

It is so easy to end up grumbling when we face pain, sadness or other difficulties. In all things, God knows what is best for us, but still we go through times when the temptation to do things our way becomes very strong.

- Are you going through a difficult time at the moment? Try not to turn away from God and his purposes. Remember his faithfulness to you, and endeavour to spend time giving thanks for that.

Session 2

God provides the things we need.

- What do you really need?
- Are there things that you have strived to obtain in your life, believing that they are necessities, that you have actually discovered to be hindrances to your Christian life? What are they? What are you going to do about them?
- Are you drawing spiritual nourishment from a relationship with Jesus?

Session 3

Prayer is not just a last resort.

- How much of a priority is prayer in your life? Is it a first or last resort?

- Do you endeavour to be organised and disciplined in prayer?

Session 4

Your spiritual leaders need your support.

- When did you last do or say something to encourage your pastor or other spiritual leaders?
- If you criticise your leaders, is it constructive criticism? And is it said in a genuinely loving and helpful way?
- Are there any practical tasks that you could do in the church that would relieve the leadership, enabling them to focus more on their spiritual responsibilities?

Session 5

Jesus wants you to be his witness.

- Are you prepared to look to Jesus to give you the wisdom, courage and enablement to do this, through the Holy Spirit?
- Will you trust the Holy Spirit to give you the right words at the right time?
- How does your daily life match up with what you profess: at home, at work, socially, in your neighbourhood, in your business and financial dealings, etc.

Session 6

God's law is all-encompassing: for the good of his creation and purposes.

- Do you believe that God's law is still applicable today?

- Are you prepared to learn its deeper significance from the teaching and example of Jesus?

- Will you allow the indwelling Holy Spirit to show you how to apply God's law to daily situations, and to enable you to put it into practice?

On a separate sheet of paper, write an action plan based on your responses to the story of Moses.

Some ideas for personal prayer

Your prayerful response to the previous section

- For the strength not to give in to temptation or to deliberately place yourself into situations of extreme temptation.

- That God will help you to follow Jesus closely and with commitment, and to not turn away from his purposes.

- For sufficient trust that God will provide your needs, and the discernment to recognise what you don't really need.

- That you will be filled with the desire to seek spiritual nourishment from a relationship with Jesus.

- For your spiritual leaders.

- To be able to fulfil your calling to witness.

- For enablement from the Holy Spirit to obey God's laws.

- Anything else that God has laid on your heart to pray about.